Fooling Around with Shakespeare

FOOLING
around with
Shakespeare

Glenda Richmond Slater

with Illustrations by
Dale Goss Mozley

Negative Capability
PRESS

Acknowledgements

HELENA INGRAM MAGRUDER (1905-1983): Take these words unto thy heart and carry them throughout thy years; I tender them to all who hear and feel the magic of the Bard.

SUE BRANNAN WALKER: Thy words they do amuse my ears; prithee write more for our enjoyment and I will see them published unto all the world.

And the other Inklings, **SUSAN MARTINELLO, SONYA BENNETT, MICKEY CLEVERDON, ROBERT O'DANIEL, MARY BETH CULP:** We are a merry band who loveth the sound of words, never failing to praise the good and pluck out the inferior.

THE PENSTERS, A WRITING GROUP: A well from whence inspiration doth spring.

BRENDA SWITALSKI: Generous hearts giveth of themselves and of their books.

HARRIET BRENNER: May gales of levity fill thy poetic sails.

MARY VAN ANTWERP (1919-2015): Write on, oh poet! Thy words do lift my soul.

KELSEY SLATER: This foolish fun doth bring forth my giggles.

CARL SLATER: Have I not urged thee always to ply thy pen? Tis I who am your fond and foremost audience.

MEGAN CARY: Who hath combined prodigious skill, artistry, and vision in assembling the book.

DALE GOSS MOZLEY: Whose whimsical quill hath captured the time, the place and the spirit of every poem.

Glenda Richmond Slater

Fooling Around with Shakespeare

© **June 2016, Glenda Richmond Slater. All rights reserved.**

Illustrations by Dale Goss Mozley, © June 2016. All rights reserved.

Cover and Interior Design by Megan Cary

ISBN: 978-0-942544-34-3
Library of Congress Control Number: 2016902783

Negative Capability Press
62 Ridgelawn Drive East
Mobile, Alabama 36608

www.negativecapabilitypress.org
facebook.com/negativecapabilitypress

To Helena Ingram Magruder

I have unclasped to thee the book even of my secret soul.
Twelfth Night

Contents

Preface

You may be long-time lover of the Bard.
You may be youth who thinks His plays too hard.
The poems you will find within this book
Provide for you a new, irreverent, look.
They focus on the foolishness and fun,
The foibles, failings, faults of fools who run
Capriciously cavorting on His pages.
These fools may be, at times, confused with sages.
I warn those who are with His plays besot:
I've taken liberties with place and plot.
Your entertainment is the peoms' intent, so
Frame thy mind to mirth and merriment!

Glenda Richmond Slater

Shakespeare's Response

Durst thou attempt to fool with my perfection?
Borrowing from here, and stealing more from there?
Think thou I'm easier played on than a pipe?
Thy rheumy rhyming shall infect my brain!

Yet still…I vow all poetry should be heard.
And there may be slight merit in thy verse.
Although thou with my plays make fast and loose,
And all is foolishness…I can but smile.

So, go to, thieving poet, flaunt my phrases!
Perhaps, at very last, thou wilt earn my praises.

A MIDSUMMER NIGHT'S SCREAM
(Fooling around with *A Midsummer Night's Dream*)

The mid of night was nigh
and temperatures were high.
Midsummer's heat beat down.
I lay in sweat-soaked gown.
No matter how I turned,
sleep, me, it seemed, had spurned,
since I put out the light
upon that fateful night.
Perhaps it's just as well,
for now I've tale to tell:

I heard small wings without,
though no birds were about.
Then came blood curdling scream.
I hoped it was a dream.
Ear-piercing call of maiden,
loud, but quickly fadin'
to whimpering small cry
that turned into a sigh.
And then there came a bray,
a deep voice saying "Nay!"

I clutched my sheet in fear.
What evil play was near?
But felt compelled to see
what had so startled me
with dire and fearful sound.
If it was still around.

I rose up from my bed,
my heart full sore with dread,
and crossed the rough-hewn floor,
and opened up my door,
and peered into the night,
and saw disgusting sight:

A donkey running there,
with flowers in his hair,
rode by a naked queen
whose eyes were flashing green.
Script that said, "I got him!"
tattooed on her bottom.

Black veils then descended.
Weird tableau was ended.
I felt that it must be
a fairy trick on me,
but knew that I must write
the strange events that night.
I rushed back to my pen
and rhymed it all, and then
I named my eerie dream
"Midsummer Night's Weird Scream"

I found it wasn't hard,
so I became a bard.

DITHERING IN DENMARK
(Fooling around with *Hamlet*)

Alas, poor Ham, I knew him well:
An ever-vacillating swell.

A prince he was, though princely not.
Too weak when things around got hot.
He dithered, couldn't take a stand;
could not dictate, nor give command.
Thought that his mum had killed his dad,
or else, he thought, his uncle had.
I ne'er was sure just what he thought;
he waffled back and forth a lot.

And also, many times, he spake
in riddles and his voice did quake.
"To be or not," he sat and pondered,
and talked to ghosts that 'round
    him wandered.

He sighed great sighs, bemoaned his life,
and ne'er got 'round to taking wife.
One fair-haired lass thought they would wed,
but he refused her from his bed,
then killed her father by mistake
to add to her severe heartache.
It caused the girl to lose her mind.
She sought out weeds that she entwined
and placed upon her fevered brow.
She sang and danced, fell in somehow
to weeping brook that bore her down.
She drowned with thistles for her crown.

This did not bother Ham a whit;
he went right on with play he'd writ.
He was no playwright, that's for sure,
but he thought play would be the cure:

forcing killer's true confession;
proving Hammie's grave obsession.
Indeed, his uncle was disturbed,
and Mum, the queen, a bit perturbed.
Alas, too late Ham drew his sword,
and Unk was not the one got gored.
The brother of the brook-took lass
slew Hammie, right there on the grass.

And now he lies here, by a friend;
two skulls together, without end.

**I dug this grave and covered him
long years ago, in times grown dim.
I oft come here to meditate
on dith'ry Hamlet's dismal fate.
It sharpens mind, it seems to me,
and broadens my philosophy.**

BUBBLE, BUBBLE
(Fooling around with *Macbeth*)

It was a murky day.
I went upon my way
to gather mushrooms in the wood;
I'd heard that they were dev'lish good.

      The wood was dark and deep.
      I heard small creatures creep
      alongside of the path I took,
      beneath the leaves that trees had shook.
      I did not fear the sound,
      but still, I looked around,
      won'dring how far I should wander;
      it was looking blacker yonder.

'Twas then I heard a shrill,
strange voice from o'er small hill.
A cackling, disagreeable,
and shout, "It's now foreseeable!"
After, came long mutter,
making me to shudder.
It spoke of murder, bloody, foul,
and ended, "Throw in beak of owl!"

      And, lo! I saw bent three:
      They looked like hags to me.
      A cauldron steamed o'er flames blazed high.
      They stirred in creature leg…
                claw…
                     eye…

My blood, it boiled with fear.
I thought that death was near.
But when I turned to run away
one hag ran after, shrieking,
                    "STAY!"

My feet stopped on the spot.
They would obey me not.
I turned and looked on wizened face
and asked, "What's happening in this place?"
My voice did quiver, quake.
My bones did shiver, shake.
The three crones cackled at my fear.
One said, "We knew that you'd come here."
I pictured in the stew
                    parts of me!
                              Quite a few!

But still I could not leave the place;
they held me in vise-like embrace.
"Your name's Macbeth, I think,"
said one. Her breath did stink.

"You thinketh wrong, you fearsome hag!
My name is Lester, Lester Flagg!
I think Macbeth is dead.
At least, that's what I've read.
Some fellow named Macduff, it's said
chopped off your poor old Mackie's head."

          "Oh drat, durn, heck," they cried.
          "Our cauldron's gone cockeyed!
          It's been predicting toil and trouble.
          Shoot, it's just been bubble, bubble.
          If you're not thane we seek,
          then prophecy we can't speak.
          The stupid kettle flubbed today;
          we won't be starring in a play!"

I turned to go, relieved.
One hag caught at my sleeve.
"Oh bide a wee," she said to me.
"Our fine concoction you must see."

I liked it not that she
was close examining me.
Especially, she eyed my eyes.
Somehow, that came as no surprise.
I snatched my arm away.
Said "Thanks, but I can't stay,"
and set out at a panicked pace
that took me swiftly from that place.

And now, whene'er I dine,
mushrooms, I decline.

LEND ME YOUR EARS
(Fooling around with *Julius Caesar*)

Listen up, sister; listen up, brother,
The Man put words together like no other.
"But it's all Greek to me," I hear you say,
talking 'bout his Julius Caesar play.
I tell you William Shakespeare's not that hard;
no, he's not heavy—he's our Bard!

I come to praise Shakespeare,
and honor him.
The words that great men write
live after them.
  So it has been with Shakespeare.

    Some folk have told you
    he's obscure and long.
    If it were so, it were a grievous fault,
    but they are wrong.

       Nay, say not, "It's all Greek to me."
       I beg, instead, you say
       you've come to listen, while
       I tell the Julius Caesar play:

Rome was a republic long ago;
It took a lot of wars to keep it so.
When mighty Julius Caesar killed Pompey
Plebs and patricians praised his victory.
But Caesar was ambitious for a crown,
So Cassius and Brutus struck him down.
Mark Antony avenged death of his friend:
Made war and Caesar's killers met their end.
Then Tony and two others took command.
They fought; two lost; Tony died by his own hand.
Just one was left, Octavius his name.
It turned out being Emperor was his aim.
He ruled the Roman Empire many years,
Thus bearing out the Brutus-Cassius fears.

   There! Shakespeare can be brief and clear, you see.
   Come back again to listen at my knee.
   Together we may pay another call
   upon the noblest writer of them all.

KING HENRY, WHO ATE
(Fooling around with *Henry VIII*)

My favorite wife of all the bunch,
(Sit down and join me in some lunch)
My best wife, as I've often said,
(Yo, lackey, fetch more loaves of bread)
The one who was the sweetest sweet,
(Mmm, mighty tempting wild boar meat)
Her name…zounds! there were such a lot,
(Bring on another full wine pot)
Well, what her name was doesn't matter,
(Let's finish up this fine cheese platter).

At any rate,

I grieve she was dispatched in haste.
She was a deal more to my taste
Than any other of my mates.
They all deserved their wretched fates.

This current queen, I thought the last,
But she is aging devilish fast.
I can't with cold crone be encumbered.
The days she'll keep her head are numbered.
She nags I live a debauched life.
I need a soft, young, comely wife.
Go, sirrah, go, and search one out
Who'll cosset me and tend my gout.

I must lie down, my ears do roar.
I ne'er have felt such pain before.
Aaargh! Fetch the leeches! In bad state!
No…skip the physic…it's too…l a
                                   t
                                    e

Of Henry, it's been often said
he died of gluttony, in his bed.
But we well know, were Henry able,
he'd have preferred to die at table.

DOUBLE TROUBLE
(Fooling around with *The Comedy of Errors*)

A merchant man from Syracuse,
with wife sailed on a pleasure cruise.
Two sets of twins were with the pair.
The question: what names should babes bear?
One set was theirs; the other, not,
but for both sets, names must be got.
They started with their own dear two;
found it a ticklish task to do.

The merchant thought Antipholus best
and nixed the names wife did suggest.
"No other name is quite as nice,
so that name will for both suffice.
Antipholus fits their high-born station."
(This merchant lacked imagination.)

  "But, surely," said his wimpish wife,
  "that will cause problems all their life."

He countered, "One good name will do.
Just call them A-One and A-Two.
Another name must still be sought
for these poor peasant twins we bought.
So let's get that out of the way;
I'm busy—haven't got all day.
They are base born, aught name will do.
We'll dub them Dromio: One and Two."

  His mate stuck to her first conclusion.
  "Same names, I think, will cause confusion.
  What if," went on this timid wife,
  "bad things should happen in their life?

"Here we are, sailing on the seas.
We each have two babes on our knees.
A fierce storm could come up and break
this ship in half, for Neptune's sake!

"We two could separated be:
A-One and D-One tied to thee,
while I would clutch, sure sore distressed,
A-Two and D-Two at my breast."

"You foolish woman!" scoffed her spouse,
"You squeak and tremble like a mouse.
Some friendly sailors sure would save
all six of us from watery grave."

"But if," she said, "some *pirates* do
pluck me, A-Two and D-Two, too,
up from the sea, cast me on shore,
and sell the boys to rich mentor,
I'd have to find a place for *me*,
perhaps in cloistered nunnery.
You might be rescued: lucky three!
Returned to Syracuse for free.
But what might happen then to you?
Now listen, for this might come true:

"What if A-One should seek his brother?
(And even, maybe, his poor mother.)
What if, with D-One he sailed 'round
and moored his ship in very town
where brother A-Two chose to dwell
and had become a rich young swell,
with waspish woman as his bride
and D-Two serving at his side?

"Two sets of twins: each looking same,
and each set sharing selfsame name!
If seen apart, it is my notion,
mix-ups could cause severe commotion.

"Two's wife might think A-One was Two
and would his actions misconstrue.
A-Two might see D-One and think
that from his orders, serf did shrink,
and beat him soundly for his slack
about the head and neck and back.
If each twin ne'er met up with bro,
I fear befuddlement would grow.

"It could become a farce of name:
a comedy of errors game!"

"That situation," Hub did say,
"could only happen in a play."
His wife spoke not another word;
as always, she to him deferred.

Then, sky turned black and waves grew high!
The thunder crashed! Bad storm was nigh!
The ship was staved, the sails were lost,
and all were in the ocean tossed!

The Merchant, with his two, did pray.
  The wife and hers were swept away.
    And loudly though the wind did blow,
      he heard her yell

I TOLD YOU SO!

THE WHALE, THE FRAIL, AND THE ALE
(Fooling around with Falstaff and Prince Henry)

Whilst traveling homeward thirstily,
the Boar's Head Tavern I did see.
Inside, a pair invited me
to drink with them—they'd pay the fee.

The fat man was a lord, said he;
the young one claimed a prince to be.
We drank at length agreeably;
then, they commenced to disagree.

> The Stout One said, "Hal, my dear boy,
> you've dealt me damned low blow!
> You've been old Falstaff's pride and joy;
> I've taught you all you know!
> Dare you swear I'm not good enough,
> you spindly Prince? You vow
> that I'm too low and coarse and rough
> to be your fellow now?
> Well, I'm *Sir* John, as well you ken,
> upraised in lordly way.
> Respected, brave, praised by all men,
> 'til drink led me astray."

> The Stripling
> said,
> "*You* taught *me?*
> *Nay*, you
> pudgy, paunchy
> Fool!
> Go!
> Lard the land!
> Be on your way.
> you
> corpulent Toadstool!"

Pot Belly yelled, "Now *Cub*, we see
you throw *your* weight around!
My Prince should never speak to me
with such base words, I'm bound."

I drew my watch. "Tis late in day,
and Sol is getting low.
Tis time to wend me on my way;
I've many miles to go."

But Falstaff grabbed me by the sleeve
and pinned me to the bench.
He said he could not let me leave,
and called for barmaid wench.

"Another round for us, my dear!"
And sure, with brimming pail,
the slattern girl did quick appear,
to pour us more stale ale.

Lean Boy said,
"Feckless,
fleshy Fool,
you prove
just what I say:
you sit and sup
and drink
and drool
at low pubs
every day."

Said Fatty, "You should not deride
your fond old Falstaff so.
You have been constant at my side;
how *else* would you this *know?*
Come, come, my fine, frail, flimsy one,
I've been your trusty tutor!
Twas I taught you to have fine fun
with cut-purse, thief and looter.
In battle, we've fought hand by hand;
you've understudied me!

You've learned to ride. Learned when to stand;
learned when it's best to flee!
I've spent long hours making you
with sword and dagger able,
but now, it seems, you've me outgrew."
His head plopped down on table.

Hal laughed.
"Drunk Whale
be right,
methinks.
We make
prodigious pair!
You stay here
now and mind
our drinks.
I'll take him
for
some air."

I sipped bad ale and did prepare
to leave on their return.
Reached for my watch. It was not there.
I felt my stomach churn.

The wench appeared, "Tis time to pay."
She handed me the chit.
I said, "I'm guest of friends today.
I do not owe a whit."

"Those two? The Whale? The Frail? They're gone.
They've stuck *you* with the bill.
No need, you mug, to carry on,
'cause ante up, *you will.*"

The ale had stole away my sense,
and I'd been sore deceived.
But Fatstuff, *lord?* Half Hal, *a prince?*
Those lies I *ne'er* believed.

Magic Show
(Fooling around with *The Tempest*)

Step right up and see the show!
Renowned magician, Prospero,
will entertain, delight, amaze,
and uplift spirits, as you gaze
in spellbound awe, in fascination,
at his prestidigitation!

A tempest rises. Ship is sunk.
But all aboard survive the dunk.
They're saved, as waves do ebb and flow,
by necromancer, Prospero.
But then, 'twas *he* who did prevail
to bring about the dreadful gale.

The passengers, flung in the sea,
include the King of Napoli;
his son, the young Prince Ferdinand,
who is his father king's right hand;
plus, evil Duke Antonio,
who usurped brother Prospero,
and exiled him, with dainty daughter,
to rocky isle in midst of water.

When banished, Prospero looked around
and saw that witchcraft did abound
amongst the crags, the rough terrain;
decided warlock's skill to gain.
He was fast learner, set his focus,
became expert at hocus-pocus.
Then did he find a new delight,
conscripting for himself a sprite:
blithe Ariel, a real whiz kid
who serves his master's every bid.
Especially, he makes up ditty
for mood that's wanted, *sad* or *witty,*
and since 'tis magic, what is more—
no one can see this troubadour!

When ship ship-wrecks in his own sea,
our Prospero is filled with glee!
To gain his Dukedom back, his plan.
Plus, suitor get for daughter's hand.
Presto! The Prince is quite a catch!
Miranda's 'bout to meet her match!

Prosp gets to work on his great notion,
calls on his sprite, sets all in motion.
The King thinks his loved son's been lost,
for he's seen him in ocean tossed.
But Ferdinand's been saved apart,
to meet the girl and lose his heart.
And she, who's seen no man but daddy,
doth lose her heart to handsome laddie.

Sly Prospero gets Ariel busy,
keeping King and Duke both dizzy:
led here and there by spritely tunes
throughout a spell-full afternoon,
with King sore grieving his "dead" son,
and Duke with fright near to undone.

So, on to Act III! Open curtain!
Things turn out well, that's for certain.
As Prospero worketh all his wiles,
we'll end this play with all 'round smiles.

He reunites the Prince and King.
King abdicates, now *Prince* is King.
King Ferd and Mandy they will pool
their talents as they Naples rule.
She's picked up magic on the isle;
he'll be a charmer with his smile.
Usurper Duke now sees the light:
he gives up Dukedom without fight.
However, we don't trust his whim;
we'll keep the evil eye on *him*.

And now, Good Audience, it is time
to take your leave of this good rhyme.
We do not look for riches, fame;
enchantment is our only aim.
But if you have enjoyed the play,
tell others what you've seen today.
And if you have some coin to spare,
just toss it in that top hat there.
It will so please illustrious bard
who has, to please you, worked so hard!

Losing it in Venice
(Fooling around with *The Merchant of Venice*)

"You have to lose some weight." This scolding from my mate
was not the first concerning fat, and I was getting sick of that.
"There's a Venetian man," she said, "I'm told will help you pounds to shed."
She waved goodbye: "I'll see you back when all those clothes are on you slack."

I took with me a map, tucked safely in my cap,
but it got wet, could not be read, and I, I needed to be fed,
and so did find a small café, but crook-backed crone did block my way.
I'd seen her somewhere else; right then, could not remember where or when.

She said, "You're hungry, dear.
This cafe's bad, I hear.
Come home with me. I have for you
a tasty, bubbly, meaty stew.
And as for your quite large behind,
the weight-loss shop I'll help you find.
I knew that you would come this way,
at just this time, this very day."
She led me to a hut.
"Here's stew; now feed your gut."
I think I et an eye, a brain,
but was too hungry to complain.
She watched me close 'til I was through
with her quite filling cauldron brew,
then said, "Come on, I'll help you find
this lose-pounds guy you have in mind."

She hailed a passing boat
and soon we were afloat.
The gondola came to a stop
in front of smelly butcher shop.
I suddenly remembered then
just where I'd seen this crone, and when.
"Twas in the woods I came on thee!
The wicked Witches! You're Witch Three!"

"Now, now, my precious boy,
this time I bring you joy.
The shed-pounds program you did choose
will help you mounds of flesh to lose.
Our Shylock, he awaits within;
he's more than eager to begin!"
She held me fast, I peered inside,
saw man with large knife at his side.
He smiled. Big teeth did show.
"Come in, Antonio!
We'll trim you and in no time flat,
get rid of that excessive fat."

"You've got it wrong, sir, no, no, no!
I'm not your friend Antonio!
My name is Lester, Lester Flagg,
and surely this is all a gag."
Shylock, he raised his knife
and I feared for my life.

I launched myself in the canal
and swam for safer, *dry* locale.
Then ran and ran, reached home at last.
From fleeing from those fiends so fast
I was but skin and bone, wet through,
exhausted, rank, and turning blue.

My wife, she held her nose.
"We'll have to burn those clothes."

"I lost the weight for you," I said,
"I'm skinny, very nearly dead."

"You've lost too much, too soon, my dear.
I don't like this new look, I fear.
But never mind, I have at hand
two cooks who'll help you re-expand."

And in walked Witches One and Two,
bearing bubbling bowl of stew.

The Play's the Thing
(Fooling around with *Richard the Third*)

Was ever good man more maligned?
More vilified by all mankind?
King Richard ruled with even hand,
brave warrior, fighting for his land.
And, striving to improve existence
for peasants living on subsistence,
he had laws changed that were unfair
to subjects dwelling in despair.
For family, he deeply cared
and with them all his largesse shared.
He kept his orphaned nephews near;
'twas clear he always loved them dear.

His means of gaining throne were just,
arresting only those he must.
For in that day, plots did abound—
King-Slayers circled all around.
The worst were those of Tudor name.
Although they had a weaker claim,
to England's throne they did aspire,
and with them, others did conspire:
Made war to make King Richard yield,
and slew him there on Bosworth Field.

The Tudors should be vast ashamed.
They did great Richard Three defame,
and "Monster" name on him they hung.
Their slander through the years hath rung:
"An evil man, a sly hunchback,
with withered arm and heart so black
he killed his nephews, banished kin.
He hath committed every sin!"
Their dastard lies caught the attention
of One whose Name I dare not mention.
He used the Tudors' false invention,
and his Play sealed misapprehension.

But others, for five hundred years,
have writ that it is all too clear
that Tudors re-wrote history,
and Richard reigned heroically.
If that darned Play is just ignored,
his reputation is restored.

IMOGEN'S DIARY
(Fooling around with *Cymbeline*)

Dear Diary, My Posthumus I wed today!
But he was caught and sent away
before we made it to a bed,
so I still have my maidenhead!
To Cymbeline, my father-King,
our marriage doesn't mean a thing.
And plotting Queen, my vile stepmother,
would marry me to *creep* stepbrother.
Oh, woe is me, alas, alack,
I want my precious Possie back!

Dear Diary, A man has come from Italy,
bringing dreadful news to me!
He says my Possie is untrue
with every woman in his view!
The man, whose name is Iachimo,
declares *he'll* be my brand new beau.
I told the fellow I thought not.
What a nerve that guy has got!

Dear Diary, The Italian was, I find, a skunk!
He hid himself inside a trunk
and to my bedroom had it taken.
When I found out, I was sore shaken.
While I slept soundly, safe and warm,
he took a bracelet from my arm.
I woke from slumber when he stole
a look at *very private* mole!
Well, he has left. I'm leaving, too.
What else is hard-pressed girl to do?

Dear Diary, This morning I got up at dawn
so I could dress and get me gone!
In boyish clothes I took disguise

and pulled cap down to hide my eyes.
To Italy I'm going to go.
I'll find my Posthumus and know
if Iachimo told truth or lie.
If it were truth, I plan to die!

Dear Diary, I got quite lost in wild Welsh wood!
I'd walked until I no more could.
A lived-in cave carved in a hill
contained cooked meat: I ate my fill.
I meant to leave 'fore cavemen came,
but was so tired, and foot was lame,
that slumber took me in its care.
I woke to find three men were there!

Dear Diary, Discovering cave has been felicitous:
the cavemen are downright solicitous!
A boy, they all b'lieved me to be
and they took quite a shine to me.
And now I don't feel so alone
because the young two are my *own*
dear brothers we thought lost forever!
They've known their royal lineage, never!

Dear Diary, So much has hap'd since I last wrote!
I'll sum it up in one quick note:
A potion made me seem quite dead.
Stepbrother lost his creepy head.
The cruel Queen got sick and died.
My Possie found his friend had lied.
There was a battle and my bro's
showed up in bravest warrior pose.
King, glad his fresh-found sons were winners,
pardoned all and sundry sinners.
I woke to find the man I'd wed!
We finally made it into bed!!!

P.S. Dear Diary, I am no longer mild and meek,
and bigger roles I now do seek!

When I was pressed on every side,
I took full charge and hit my stride!
I tell them all with tongue grown glib,
I'm organizing Ladies' Lib!

P.P.S. Dear Diary, The King let Iachimo go free,
in spite of what he'd pulled on me!
That blighter is so evil-hearted,
a School for Scoundrels he has started!

All the World's My Stage
(Fooling around with *As You Like It*)

My first words were "I'll be a star!"
Mum said, "No Jack…be what you are,
and as a farmer, you'll go far."
But acting was the dream I had,
not farming, like my dear, dead dad.
Dirt did not do a thing for me.
I wanted all the world to see
me on the stage, up there in lights:
in love scenes tender, fierce in fights.
Alas, it did not work that way.
I couldn't find the perfect play.

When just an infant, I was cast
as puking, mewling short-lived lass.

My whining school boy never gelled;
the part was cut and I, "expelled."

And though I languished,
mooned and sighed,
my lover role all did deride.

"You have no talent Jack, you blob,"
dear Mummy said. "Go get a job
and help me feed your hungry gob."
But I ignored her gloomy sighs;
I knew one day my star would rise.

I grew a beard and looked much bolder,
auditioned for a fearsome soldier.
Never been rejected quicker.
Thought I heard one of them snicker.

"I'm getting old," dear Mummy said,
"and still you're here and must be fed.
You're aging too, you lie-a-bed."

White was my beard, my belly round.
Ah! Old men parts seemed to abound!
But *this* is all *I* got to play:
a Santa Claus. For half a day.

And then my voice did sadly change,
with only high notes in its range.
My eyes they dimmed,
my legs they shrunk,
my hearing went…*but not my spunk!*

Dear Mummy's gone now, so I dwell
in geriatric, cheap hotel.
But still my hopes within me swell.
To be a star remains my scheme—
sans faculties, but not sans *dream.*

Racking up Rhymes
(Fooling around with *Othello*)

I'm Iago! I'm a villain,
and widely known for that!
I've out-villained all the others
who have worn the villain's hat!
I should have had a statuette
proclaiming my great role!
Instead, the fools arrested me
and stuck me in this hole.

They come each day with instruments
of torture, which they wield
with delectation and delight,
but they can't make me yield.
In fact, I quite enjoy the game
and when they're gone, at night,
it does inspire material for
the poetry that I write.

Aha! you didn't know that I
am poet without peer!
Well, that's what caused the problems
that have landed me in here.
I'm telling *all* quite brilliantly
in my spell-binding verse.
Sit back and listen to me now
while I recite:

"My Curse"
They call me a villain; "a monster," they say
and blame me for everyone's wrongs,
but all that I wanted, throughout the whole play
was to write witty poems and songs.

Othello the Moor could not talent discern;
his thoughts were of war and brute strength.

A primitive man who a verse could not learn,
　　but could tell tales of battle at length.
I offered to put his great stories in rhyme,
　　to be sung, at occasions, by me.
He said that my job was to spend all my time
　　plotting upcoming battles at sea.
I thought if I had only option to fight,
　　I should be, at the least, his first mate.
When he lifted Cassio up to that height,
　　he turned my contempt into hate.

Had this been the end of the slightings I bore,
　　I might have just swallowed my pride
and served out my tour (it was three years; no more)
　　by barbarian Moor's boorish side.
But his wife, Desdemona, made sport of my verse
　　when I tried to amuse her one day.
She said it was impotent, foolish, and worse.
　　Well, that's when my hatred took sway.

The Moor was, in spite of his prowess in war,
　　insecure in his low social rating.
Des's dad said their marriage was simply bizarre;
　　and he'd never approve of the mating.
Then I, in revenge, told Othello I'd heard
　　that Cassio had bedded his wife.
The fool thought me honest, believed every word.
　　(He'd been gullible all of his life.)

But ne'er did I think he'd go crazy that way
　　because of the flames that I fanned:
that his brown eyes would morph into green, and that day
　　Desdemona would die by his hand.
Nor that, when he learned she was blameless—too late—
　　he would find a sharp knife on the shelf,
and proclaiming his guilt, and her innocent state,
　　plunge the knife in his miserable self.

It wasn't my fault that the Moor went berserk
and his wife was too timid to run.
But they say it was caused by my "foul, dirty work,"
and they come to my dungeon for fun.
They torment and torture me by every means:
the rack and the thumbscrews and such.
I plead and I scream and I say they're obscene,
but they really don't hurt me that much.

Ah! The epic I'll write will make all see the light.
I'm composing it during my dreams.
'Twill establish my innocence, show I was right.
'Twas *Othello* who went to extremes.

TOO MUCH ADO
(Fooling around with *Much Ado About Nothing*)

In sonnets, Ben and Bea swore enmity.
Said they, "On friendly terms, we'll never be."

Benedick's Sonnet to Beatrice
Shall I compare thee to a summer's day?
Lord no, more like December's gale, you be.
Your rough squalls blow all pleasant thoughts away,
And every blast is aimed from you to me.
Sometime all cold your visage doth appear
And words that blare from off your biting tongue,
Like hailstones pounding down around my ear,
Sometime do sting a bit when they are flung.
But thy infernal winter chills me not.
I match thee tit for tat in repartee.
I give back just as good as I have got,
And never fail with you to disagree.
    So long as I can breathe, have tongue for use,
    So long will I deflect your cold abuse.

Beatrice's Sonnet to Benedick
Shall I compare thee to a summer's day?
Lord no, more like a March wind's blow you be.
You howl 'bout enemies you've swept away,
And blast us with your every victory.
Sometime quite hot your visage doth appear
When you have felt a blast from my quick tongue.
Still, blustery words do fall about my ear;
You trumpet on, e'en when I know you're stung.
But thy raw, rowdy spring is huff and puff.
I laugh at tales of your exploits in war,
Decrying all reports as merest bluff,
And winning every point as we do spar.
    So long as I can breathe, have tongue to use,
    So long will I your ego sore abuse.

Yet, plotting cupids looked at them and said
That they were clearly meant, these two, to wed.

The Prince, with Claudio, Ben's dearest friend,
Concocted plot to bring about that end.
They told Ben that fair Bea did love him dear,
But that rejection was her greatest fear.

Then they enlisted help from women folk
Who thought that it would be a bonny joke
To tell Bea that brave Ben did love her dear,
But that rejection was *his* greatest fear.

It worked a charm. Both took the hearsay bait
And shortly wound up in the married state.
They said their fierce façade had been all wrong;
They'd liked each other right well all along.

ALAS

Poor Ben and Bea weren't made to coo.
Each found it hard their brand new mate to woo.
They did not like to bow and scrape and smile.
Soft answers and caresses weren't their style.

Yet still, they tried. They spoke with sweetened words.
They sang love songs and kissed like two tame birds.
Until they found their lives become so dulled,
Both wanted marriage rites to be annulled.

The Prince did hear their case, then said, with smile,
That they should stick together for a while.
He told them, "Put the lovey-dove away;
Go back to being your true selves today."

The Prince was wise; he gave them sage advice.
They quickly quit false roles of making nice.

Who Takes the Rap?
(Fooling around with *King Lear*)

Old King Lear was a weary old Lear, and wanted to retire.
Advisers were against it, said "Hold on, King! Where's the fire?"
His Fool told him he suffered from advanced senility.
Lear didn't pay them any mind; he called his daughters, three.
He told the gals he wanted each to take part of the realm;
    then he would take it easy
      with his children at the helm.

"But first," said Lear, "I need to hear just which one loves me best.
She'll get most of the kingdom and the others get the rest."
Fierce Regan and foul Goneril, they did a song and dance:
They flattered him with bald-faced lies and made most of their chance.
He smiled and nodded and approved their hypocritic speech,
    then asked, "Cordelia, what say you,
      my favorite little peach?"

She would not stoop to flattery to get part of the booty,
but said she loved him just as much as was a daughter's duty.
The King told Cordy on her words large part of kingdom hung.
Told her, "Say more, Cordelia! Or has some cat got your tongue?"
But she was stubborn and refused to speak another word.
    The King was just plain furious
      at what he *hadn't* heard.

So she got disinherited and told "To France with you!"
He gave his kingdom then and there to the wicked other two.

The Fool told King, "You've lost your mind and you'll regret this day!"
Lear, he refused to listen; in fact, ordered him away.
Well, Fool, he scarpered off and in an alley he did hide,
but next day he was back again, right by the old King's side.

In no time flat, proud Lear found out he'd been a good bit rash.
Cruel daughters both turned him away. They treated him like trash.

The Fool said, "Hey, I told you so!" (That guy just would not shut up.)
Lear yelled at him he'd banished be, if the hounding didn't let up.
King wandered his old stomping grounds in extreme mental pain.
When youngest daughter heard of this, well, she turned up again.

The Fool feared for her safety, but 'course she, hard-headed kid,
paid not a bit of mind to him. (Nobody ever did.)

Foul sisters hated Cordy and they didn't want her 'round.
Soon,
        dangling
            from
                a
            doorway,
                she
                was
by her daddy found.
This loss of favorite daughter, it did make the King dire sad,
and it was plain to all the 'hood that he was taken bad.

Those evil sisters, since they had the hots for selfsame guy,
did plot against each other, and quite soon each one did die.

You'd think that Lear would step up then, and back his kingdom win,
but no, that didn't happen, 'cause of weird shape he was in.
The old guy shucked off all his clothes and to a field did run.
He took no notice, in his grief, that fierce storm had begun.
He moaned and groaned and carried on and cursed his hapless fate,
while rain and hail poured down upon his hatless, hairless pate.

Fool never missed a chance to say, "Hey King, I told you so,"
and everywhere old Lear did roam, that Fool was sure to go.
When finally the King expired, bare-naked in the rain,
his Fool was right there, more than glad to rub it in again.

. . . .

Psychologists do not agree on what destroyed Lear's mind.
They muse, they study, argue, as they seek the cause to find.
Some say that it was all his fault: the prideful, stubborn mule.
But others say his brain gave out from nagging by that Fool.

Is Love Blind?
(Fooling around with *Twelfth Night*)

A tempest beat upon a boat
and tossed these twins in Triton's moat:
Sebastian and Viola. They
were from each other swept away.
Each thrashed and for their sibling sought,
and each were drowned, so other thought.

Viola, when washed up on shore,
was led by seaman to the door
of handsome Count who needed Page.
She'd dressed as boy and looked fair sage;
took for herself a laddie's name.
"Cesár" was who young Vi became.

The Count was pleased and spurned her not;
forsooth, he hired her on the spot.
She took one look and went all hot.
Love at first sight—that were her lot.
She thought him sent her from above!
Alas, *another* was his love.
And, far as Count knew, Vi were *lad.*
For sure, that's how the lass were clad.

The first thing Count would have Page do:
take to rich Countess billet-doux.
When Countess saw "Cesár's" fine face,
she fell in love with "him" apace.
I tell you, it were fair a mess;
Vi ne'er should worn a laddie's dress.

Meanwhile, Sebastian washed up, too,
along with captain from ship's crew.

Cap said he'd go and look around.
Seb also wandered through the town,
and what he wore—list' you to this—
was just like tunic worn by Sis!

Well now it even gets more strange.
The Countess saw Seb at close range
and thought he was the handsome Page
for whom her heart with love did rage.
She hugged and kissed him quite a lot.
Proposed to him right on the spot.

He, being lost and without money,
decided she was quite the honey.
He didn't pause nor hesitate
to enter into married state.

The bridegroom and his new-took bride
went to see Count (Page at Count's side),
announced their nuptials to all there,
and this the Count could hardly bear.
Vi 'fessed up then, in girl's voice clear,
that she were lass and loved him dear.
Count stood amazed and swore, by gad,
she'd always looked, to him, a lad!
Then, being fairly fickle sort,
he took fair Vi as his consort.

Thus, Vi and Seb each other found,
each happy t'other hadn't drowned.

When told this tale, I pondered some,
and to conclusion I did come:
This mixing up of lads and lasses
might well be cured by well-fit glasses.

CORRALLING KATE
(Fooling around with *The Taming of the Shrew*)

There was a filly, name of Kate,
    that never had been broke.
She was a rough one, this gal was
    and easy to provoke.
She had a wicked right-left jab
    and vicious tongue, to boot.
She'd out-rope, out-ride all the guys
    and any guy, out-shoot.
All us cowpokes hereabouts
    had felt her heavy hand.
We crossed the street when she went by;
    she'd never wear *our* brand.

A cowboy who had lost his job
in a traveling Wild West Show
knew this Kate had a thriving ranch.
His name? Tex Truchio.
Tex moseyed into town one day,
his sights set on a wife,
and reckoned Kate was just the one
to bankroll his new life.

    His sidekicks called him "Loco Tex"
    when his plan got around
    to court the wild, rambunctious Kate,
    get yoked, and settle down.
    They warned him not to marry her.
    "She can't be broke," they said.
    "You're wrong there, boys," was his reply,
    "She's just been poorly bred.
    Her father was a'feared of her.
    He should've tanned her hide.
    I'll break that filly quick," he bragged,
    "when she's my blushing bride."

He let no grass grow underfoot,
called scowling Kate his Darling,
and acted like a laid back sort
who'd not be one for quarreling.
So she said, "What the heck—I need
more muscle on my spread."
Her answer was to lasso Tex
and haul him off to wed.

As soon as they had said their vows
he shed that meek disguise.
Became downright tyrannical,
right there before her eyes.
He set in quick to tame his bride:
refused to let her eat.
Said all the grub was poorly cooked,
not good enough for his Sweet.
She, weak from hunger, tried to sleep;
this too, he did forbid.
Was always there to wake her up
no matter where she hid.

Well, after weeks of misery
at Tex's big strong hand,
poor Kate was just plumb tuckered out,
was broken, like he'd planned.
She then got sleep and *lots* of grub
and ate so much that she
gained fifty pounds…well, maybe more:
wore X-LARGE, finally.

Tex Truchio rode forth to shout
he'd tamed his cowgirl shrew.
He didn't notice when his wife
grew…and grew…and grew…
As soon as she was big and strong
she did what she'd planned all along.

She hogtied him, said, "You're demoted,
and back to Queen Kate, I'm promoted!"

> He struggled, pleaded. She just laughed.
> "I'm taking over, Toad.
> If you don't like the way it is,
> well, Truchio, there's the road."

> The poor fool looks for sympathy
> from his old sidekick crew.
> He cries, bemoans his hen-pecked life
> and asks what can he do?
> They say, "You shoulda listened, Pard.
> You rushed in, willy-nilly.
> The fact is that it's *you* that's broke.
> It sure ain't Kate, the filly!"

ALL'S NOT WELL
(Fooling around with *All's Well That Ends Well*)

My father taught me medicine.
"Dear Helena," he said,
"when I am gone, you'll take my place."
Too soon, dear Dad were dead.
A kindly Countess took me in:
a grateful orphan, I.
She loved me like a daughter and
her son were cutie pie!
His mother dearly wished that he,
Bert, would return my love,
but he said I was far beneath,
and he, too far above.

And then, word came the King were sick;
expected soon to die.
I gathered herbs that very day
and to the Court did hie.
My skill were great, my medicines worked;
soon King were up and fine.
And grateful! He said he would grant
the fondest wish of mine!
Of course I said I wanted most
dear Bertram for my groom.
Bert did decline, but King decreed:
we wed, Bert glum with gloom.
He did refuse to bed me and
he fled that very night.
It seemed he wanted nothing but
to be out of my sight.

I went home to the Countess and
received a note from Bert.
I cried, it were so hateful.
Bert sure knew how to hurt.

He wrote "When I give you the ring
that I have worn forever,
I'll call you wife and live with you,
but that will happen, NEVER!"
I went, alone, on pilgrimage;
in Florence, stayed at inn.
Found out my Bert had been there, too!
That made my head fair spin.

Landlady said, not only that,
he'd come to woo and wed
her daughter, Di, a comely lass.
He thought that I were dead!
When those two heard my tale of woe,
they dressed me in Di's gown
and doused me with her perfume.
When Bert came sneaking round,
I used her voice in pitch black room.
He was completely fooled:
thought I was Di, called me his love
said over him I ruled.
It were a dark and stormy night—
we spent it all in bed.
I got the ring from off his hand!
He'd marry me, he said.

Next morning, he found out 'twas I:
his real bride, and alive.
He vowed that he would stay with me,
but now he doth contrive
to be at Court most of the time,
while I the children rear.
I'm also busy with my herbs;
in fact, I've famed career.
Friends ask, "Why let him treat you thus?
You are a woman grown!"
They tell me there is help for me,
that I am not alone.

An English princess, Imogen,
they say, leads women's band.
(I like its name: The Ladies' Lib.)
They say she'll lend a hand.
And there's a woman, name of Kate.
Her husband was a rover,
but now he's tethered at her side.
They say to ask her over.
They also say, "See Lester Flagg,"
because they have a notion
that three hags that he sees a lot
might stir up a love potion.
If all else fails, they say to go
to Oz: it is well-known
a wizard there has body parts.
He'll give me a backbone!

Snake Charmer
(Fooling around with *Antony and Cleopatra*)

Every once in a while,
on the serpentine Nile,
as it wends its way
north to the sea,
a dim outline's seen:
Royal Barge of a Queen,
and in silence it floats, eerily.
Apparition, it seems,
from out shadowy dreams.
An old man tells its story to me:

Queen Cleopatra was a vamp
who broke a lot of hearts.
Not only did she have the looks,
she also had the smarts.

She reigned with strong and skilful hand,
her voice was soft and sweet.
Her talents and her beauty
set all Egypt at her feet.

The asp was royal symbol and
fair Cleo loved her snakes.
She kept them close beside her for,
she said, good Fortune's sake.
She daily cruised the winding Nile
in golden, perfumed barge.
Twas all decked out in purple and
amenities were large.

But soon, alas, dire trouble struck:
in Egypt things turned bad.
Disease and famine, locusts, wars,
and quarrels with Rome they had.

To Caesar, desperate Cleo went,
concealed within a rug.
When she unrolled her comeliness,
he wrapped her in a hug.
He swore that he'd protect her
and her country with his life,
and he did, 'til cunning cohorts
killed great Caesar with a knife.

Mark Antony was Caesar's friend,
lieutenant in his fights,
so Cleo made a

       zig

           zag

    move

and set *him* in her sights.
Love fatally did strike them both,
her barge, their wooing ground:
gliding on the winding Nile
while snakes around *them* wound.
They planned to conquer all of Rome,
but lost on sea and land.
When Cleo saw they vanquished were,
she grabbed her snakes and ran.
Her Love was told that she was dead:
the woman he adored.
He wept and wailed in anguish
and
then
fell
upon
his
sword.

Proud victor of the Roman wars
(Octavius, his name)
was immunized to Cleo's charms
and planned her public shame.

Brave female Pharaoh, she did choose
the end that best befit her.
She made her serpents hissing mad
and on her breast they bit her.

She was applauded, lauded,
for the royal way she died.
And now she glides
on ghostly barge,
two adders at her side.

ROMEO AND JULIET BUY THE FARM
(Fooling around with *Romeo and Juliet*)

The Montagues and Capulets,
for fifty year or more,
wuz feudin' and afightin' and
them hills wuz filled with gore.

Young Romeo wuz Montague
and Juliet, a Cappy,
but when they met and danced a jig
they both got moon-eyed sappy.

Romy said, "Let's us get hitched!"
and Julie said, "Why, shore!"
They rushed off to a preacher man.
Right then their vows they swore.

The two snuck into Julie's room
to spend their weddin' night.
They had to make it quick so he
could scram at first daylight.

Next day, the groom was roamin' round
with kinfolk at his side,
and the durn fool killed a guy who wuz
first cousin to his bride.
His pals told him, "You gotta git!
Make tracks, for your neck's sake!"

He went back to the preacher.
That was a big mistake.
"You head for them thar hills," Preach said,
"to hole up somewhere, chile,
til things cool down amongst them Caps.
It may take quite a while."

But Julie's pa found her a beau,
a city slicker lad.
Pa said, "It's time you married up,

You *are* fourteen, by gad."
He said they wuzn't gonna wait;
the next day wuz the weddin' date.
The pore gal wuz already hitched,
but couldn't 'fess up to it.
She asked that preacher man to help
and he rushed in to do it.
He had her take and chug-a-lug
some strong white lightnin' brew,
and she *looked* like she'd bought the farm,
but law, that wuzn't true.

Romeo, he got the word
(bad news shore travels fast)
that Juliet had tooken sick
and breathed her very last.
He took off like a scalded dog
to see what he could do,
stopping only once—to get
a jug of mountain dew.

When he got to the buryin' vault,
seen Julie lookin' dead,
he swallered all that moonshine up
and died there, at her head.
Well, she woke up, saw him there stiff,
grabbed up his knife right quick,
and shoved that shiv straight through her heart—
whoo boy, *that* done the trick!

Well, one good thang come outta this:
them families stopped their feud.
They've got together, thick as thieves,
to have that preacher sued.

ANNUAL SPONSORS

EDITOR'S CIRCLE
Dr. Charles & Mary Rodning
Drs. Ron & Sue Walker
James & Megan Honea
Barry Marks, Esq.

SUSTAINING SPONSORS
Dr. Vivian Shipley
Nathan Blaesing

SUPPORTING SPONSORS
Steve & Dora Rubin
Eric and Kimberly Rubin
Kristina Marie Darling

CONTRIBUTING SPONSORS
Nicole Amare
Dr. Betty Ruth Speir
Phyllis Feibelman
Harry & Dorothy Riddick
Gaylord Brewer

ABOUT SPONSORSHIP

Since 1981 Negative Capability Press has been committed to publishing quality books of exciting and innovative poetry, fiction, and nonfiction. We are a 501(c)(3) tax-exempt nonprofit organization and are designated by the State of Alabama as a Domestic Nonprofit Corporation. Our press is managed by a volunteer collective dedicated to independent publishing. Every dollar we earn is put directly back into our press – whether it is publishing our next book, marketing our authors, maintaining our website or increasing our distribution opportunities. It is you, our valued supporters, that will allow us to continue to publish beautiful, innovative books by amazing authors. We appreciate your support!

ANNUAL SPONSORSHIP LEVELS

Contributing Sponsor - $50–$99 per year
Acknowledged on our website and in our publications.

Supporting Sponsor - $100–$249 per year
Acknowledgment, plus a limited edition broadside.

Sustaining Sponsor - $250–$499 per year
Acknowledgment, limited edition broadside, plus a signed book.

Editor's Circle - $500 and up
Acknowledgment, limited edition broadside, signed book and an invitation to our salon readings.

Donations may be made at www.negativecapabilitypress.org/donate or by sending a check to:
Negative Capability Press, 62 Ridgelawn Dr. E, Mobile, AL 36608